You Don't Have to Be Smart to Walk With God

How to Recognize the Voice of God

You Don't Have to Be
Smart to Walk With God

How to Recognize the Voice of God

Dale M. Sides

Treasure House
An Imprint of
Destiny Image
P.O. Box 310
Shippensburg, PA 17257

"For where your treasure is
there will your heart be also." Matthew 6:21

ISBN 1-56043-830-4

For Worldwide Distribution
Printed in the U.S.A.

Treasure House books are available through these fine distributors outside the United States:

Christian Growth, Inc.
Jalan Kilang-Timor, Singapore 0315

Lifestream
Nottingham, England

Rhema Ministries Trading
Randburg, South Africa

Salvation Book Centre
Petaling, Jaya, Malaysia

Successful Christian Living
Capetown, Rep. of South Africa

Vision Resources
Ponsonby, Auckland, New Zealand

WA Buchanan Company
Geebung, Queensland, Australia

Word Alive
Niverville, Manitoba, Canada

Inside the U.S., call toll free to order:
1-800-722-6774

To the Reader

Please read this book in the attitude of worship, not in the attitude of learning. This is not just the author speaking to you; these are words to inspire your worship and your acknowledging that God is speaking to you.

Contents

Introduction

The first verse of an old hymn, "My God and I," expresses a personal, intimate relationship with God.

My God and I go in the fields together;
We walk and talk as good friends should and do.
We clasp our hands; our voices ring with laughter.
My God and I go through the meadow's hue.

This hymn conveys what it means to intimately "walk with God." The relationship is developed as you spend time in conversation with your heavenly Father. Fellowship means a full sharing of hearts with each other. You share your innermost feelings with God and He speaks tenderly to you.

Communication with God is more than people praying to Him; God also speaks to His people. This is an integral part of their relationship with God. After all, the Bible documents

God's speaking from cover to cover. But it seems that most children of God are more adept in talking to God than they are in listening to Him and recognizing when He speaks. Many Christians enjoy the privilege of taking things to God in prayer, but not the great joy and benefit in listening to an answer from Him.

The purpose of this book is to explore this intimate relationship with God and to reveal the simplicity of how He communicates with you. More specifically, the primary consideration will be *how* to listen to God and distinguish when He speaks to you.

Christians should always remember that God formed, made, and created mankind for the purpose of fellowship. God wants to walk and talk with His people. This is God's idea, not something that believers have to convince Him to do. Since God wants fellowship, He has not saddled the believer with endless stipulations and qualifications required for engaging in this relationship. This is the simple relationship between the loving heavenly Father and His child.

The simplicity of walking and talking with God lies in acknowledging that He is your Father and He is love. Would it be very loving of the Father to make it complicated for His children to hear Him? Why would God want to have children if He could not have a warm, sweet, loving, simple relationship with them? Does it make sense that God would give the ultimate sacrifice of Jesus Christ to have children and then make it difficult to communicate with them?

God has revealed Himself in and speaks to His people through His written Word. The written Word of God is the basis for all relationships; yet, is there not a personal relationship available with Him, too? Does God not have the capacity to personally speak to His people?

The Scriptures tell of men and women who walked with God and followed His specific directions. Is this not available now? Did God send Jesus Christ to reconcile people only to tell them to read about Him in a book? Did He not send Jesus Christ to reconcile people to Himself so they could have the gift of the holy spirit and develop an intimate relationship with Him?[1]

Why do Christians think they must wait until they are "smart" enough before they can begin developing a relationship with God? Earthly parents do not wait until children are grown up to begin speaking to and teaching their children. They begin talking to the baby the day he is born. The parents' commitment to teach older children is not greater than that for newborns. The relationship may be different because the older child's abilities to communicate might be more highly developed, but a loving parent is faithful to patiently teach each child regardless of the level of development. The instruction of a younger child may require more simplicity and repetition, while the teaching of an older child can be more in-depth.

Would the God of all love be any less than an earthly parent? Is He not willing and able to do as much for His children?

---

1.   The gift of the holy spirit will be designated by using lowercase letters in "holy spirit," as opposed to capital letters to indicate God, the Holy Spirit.

God works with you at your level of spiritual maturity and understanding. He communicates with all His children, regardless of age, education, or ethnic or social background. God is your Father and your Teacher. He is committed to helping you develop your relationship with Him because He desires to walk and talk with you. God lovingly and patiently works with you in order that a more meaningful and intimate relationship might develop.

The qualifications for having this walking and talking relationship with God are quite minimal. There are no educational requirements or necessary diplomas. God made each of His children able to enjoy this relationship through Jesus Christ.

Jesus saith unto him, I am the way, the truth, and the life: no man cometh unto the Father, but by Me (John 14:6).

Every child of God is qualified to walk and talk with God because He is no respecter of persons (see Acts 10:34). The truth that God is no respecter of persons has echoed through the ages; after all, God loves everyone (see Jn. 3:16). This truth communicates the fact that God does not make something available to one person while denying it to another. He shows no partiality when making His goodness and grace available. He gives each of His children access to Himself— and thereby the spiritual ability to walk and talk with Him. It is not a matter of mental ability, but of having a spiritual connection with God. This connection with God is the gift of the holy spirit.

Then Peter said unto them, Repent, and be baptized every one of you in the name of Jesus Christ for the

remission of sins, and ye shall receive the gift of the
Holy Ghost [holy spirit] (Acts 2:38).

God has made the same gift of the holy spirit available to everyone through Jesus Christ (see Eph. 2:18). Included within this gift is the spiritual ability necessary to communicate with God. This gift of the holy spirit is God's gift to all who believe on Jesus Christ. All who confess that Jesus is Lord and believe in their hearts that God raised Him from the dead receive this gift (see Rom. 10:9). Have you confessed and believed? If so, you are smart enough to walk and talk with God because you have received the spiritual ability to communicate with Him. The gift of the holy spirit gives each child the spiritual access to his Father through which this communication may take place.

The title *You Don't Have to Be Smart to Walk With God* is intended to imply simplicity. Simplicity in our relationship with God is something we should always remember and closely guard.

But I fear, lest by any means, as the serpent beguiled Eve through his subtilty, so your minds should be corrupted [away] *from the simplicity that is in Christ* (2 Corinthians 11:3).

The Greek origin of the word *simplicity* offers an interesting understanding to this discussion. *Simplicity* comes from a word that means "to plait" or "to braid." This notion implies taking a number of items and arranging them into a simple unit. It further means to take many aspects and make them "one."

This analogy of "braiding" or "plaiting" is the approach that we will use in studying how to develop a walking and talking relationship with God. Four aspects will be covered. They are separate, yet blended together they become one. These four strands include: Be Strong in Grace (Chapter 1); Be Humble (Chapter 2); Stay Your Mind on God (Chapter 3); Accept That God Works Within You (Chapter 4).

The essential matter of this study is Chapter 4, "Accept That God Works Within You." Although it appears inviting to jump directly ahead to this portion, it is not advisable. The topics of Chapters 1, 2, and 3 are fundamental to accepting the simplicity of Chapter 4. The chapters are ordered in a proper sequence to offer the most concise yet detailed instruction.

There may be methods other than the one of braiding these four subjects together that could be used to accomplish the same result. These four strands are not intended to be exclusive of other aspects. However, these four have not been chosen randomly or whimsically, but according to the "scope" of the Scriptures to thoroughly cover this subject. Regardless of the approach taken to cover this vital subject of "walking and talking with God," it is very important to remember this: *It is simple.*

You Don't Have to Be Smart to Walk With God because He, as your Father and Teacher, is smarter than you. He will lead you and help you to understand when He is talking to you. The following 25 words will serve as a touchstone and reminder of simplicity throughout this study:

Stay simple. Be strong in grace. Be humble. Stay your mind on God. Accept that He works within you. Ask God. He will teach you.

Chapter 1

Be Strong in Grace

The truths concerning God's grace almost defy descrip-
tion. Man has difficulty explaining God's grace, but God's
explanation is simple: "For God so loved that He gave" (see
Jn. 3:16). Only God's love has an expanse greater than God's
grace. Actually, God's love and grace are inseparable—God's
love is His heart and motive in blessing His people; grace is the
action whereby this boundless love is demonstrated.

God initially created mankind to fill the void of fellowship. Can you imagine being the loving, benevolent Creator
and having no one upon whom to bestow your blessings?
God, therefore, created mankind to have fellowship with
Him and to be the recipients of His loving affection and
grace.

Grace is the Greek word *charis*. Briefly, this means a gift
that is unearned. God's grace is therefore defined as God's
unmerited, divine favor to mankind. Grace demonstrates

God's unconditional love toward mankind. It is manifested in His loving commitment to pursue fellowship with His people. Anywhere fellowship with God is enjoyed, it is built upon the foundation of God's unmerited giving.

No Christian believer has ever lived such a good life that fellowship with God was earned. Likewise, no believer has been so bad that fellowship with God has been denied. Grace is the foundation upon which all relationships with God are built.

Can you fathom that God loves you enough to desire your company? Can you accept that God's divine design for you is to be His companion? Is it conceivable that the same God, Who with the sweep of His hand stretched out the heavens, would want to walk and talk with you? Can you imagine that this same God wants to make you the recipient of His affection and grace? Why not? "Hath not the potter power over the clay" (Rom. 9:21a)?

This is the lesson of grace in learning to walk and talk with God—that God wants you to be His companion; that He wants you to receive His love and enjoy His fellowship. By accepting God's grace, you can claim your worthiness to be His companion in fellowship.

The message of grace is urgently emphasized through Scripture. Every one of the seven church epistles (Romans through Thessalonians) addressed to the church to which we belong, opens with this: *"Grace to you."* This introductory salutation of each epistle helps establish that grace is the beginning of an intimate relationship with God.

Grace is the foundation of true Christian living. You can never fall so far that it will not be beneath you; nor can you rise so high that it will not be over you. Grace is where you begin, and it must always be where you continue to stand.

Thou therefore, my son, be strong in the grace that is in Christ Jesus (2 Timothy 2:1).

Standing in grace is standing on holy ground. This holy ground was won by Jesus Christ; now it must be diligently guarded by believers. It should come as no surprise to learn that there is a constant battle to annul the effect of grace and the goodness of God. This plot of "holy ground" is constantly under siege. Every believer must confront the truth that he is in a spiritual battle. To preserve the truth of grace, every believer must decide if his worth is based upon God's goodness or on his own works of self-justification. This precious ground must never be relinquished to the onslaughts of the adversary. Grace must be the headquarters and stronghold for all Christian believers. It is the foundation upon which all other aspects of a relationship with God are built.

Grace, therefore, is the first strand in the braid of simplicity of walking and talking with God. All other aspects of this relationship must be woven into this fundamental and primary truth.

Perhaps the most well-known verse of Scripture is John 3:16. This verse proclaims the grace of God with His sending Jesus Christ into the world to rescue people. God acted upon His nature of love and compassion by making the advanced payment for any and all. This verse, perhaps more than most others, wonderfully declares the grace of God.

For God so loved the world, that He gave His only begotten Son, that whosoever believeth in Him should not perish, but have everlasting life (John 3:16).

In order for you to become God's child and companion, God paid the price of His Son, Jesus Christ. By grace, and only by grace, God rescued you out of the kingdom of this world. You were born into this world without God and without hope until the almighty hand of God snatched you out of the clutches of despair. He purchased you with the life of His only begotten Son. God made you righteous and justified you. Now, as God's child, you have been made worthy to stand in His presence in righteousness and true holiness.

All of these things were accomplished because of God's love and grace for you. These wonderful blessings did not come because you deserved them, but simply because God desired your fellowship.

God sent Jesus Christ to be the payment in order to make grace available for you.

For all have sinned, and come short of the glory of God; being justified freely by His grace through the redemption that is in Christ Jesus: whom God hath set forth to be a propitiation through faith in His blood, to declare His righteousness for the remission of sins that are past, through the forbearance of God; to declare, I say, at this time His righteousness: that He might be just, and the justifier of him which believeth in Jesus (Romans 3:23-26).

The opposite of being justified by the grace of God is trying to be justified by one's own works. This poses a great problem for believers desiring to develop a relationship with God. When anyone thinks he can earn a relationship with God through his own works, then he will also believe that he could be denied the same privilege by a lack of good works. The Word of God speaks clearly on this topic.

For by grace are ye saved through faith; and that not of yourselves: it is the gift of God: not of works, lest any man should boast (Ephesians 2:8-9).

There is no boasting in salvation or in the walk with God after salvation because grace is the foundation for a relationship with God. The basis of this relationship is God's goodness, not man's worthiness.

Where is boasting then? It is excluded. By what law? of works? Nay: but by the law of faith (Romans 3:27).

Grace is the message that tells believers they are righteous and justified. One's own works neither merit a relationship with God nor deny one. When Christian believers do not know or refuse to accept the teaching of grace, they feel too unworthy to have a fellowship with God. They look at their own works and realize that they fall miserably short of worthiness. This feeling of unworthiness is the main reason believers do not accept that God works within them (Chapter 4). They question why God would want to talk to someone of their lowly stature. This feeling constantly puts them under pressure to do certain things to earn their worthiness. Because no one can earn the worthiness to walk and talk with God, believers can easily fall into the grip of condemnation.

Verily, verily, I [Jesus Christ] *say unto you, he that heareth My word, and believeth on Him that sent Me, hath everlasting life, and shall not come into condemnation; but is passed from death unto life* (John 5:24).

Jesus Christ promised that all who believed on Him would not have to suffer condemnation. Condemnation is the Greek word *katakrino*. It is composed of *kata*, "down" and *krino*, "judge." It means to put someone down. This is being judged, or put down, by someone else, or "judging yourself" or "putting yourself down." Since God is the Judge and Jesus Christ has sworn not to condemn a believer, the "putting down of one's own self" is the self-condemnation that strangles believers. This happens when believers assess their worth according to their own works and not according to what God made them through Jesus Christ's works. Not claiming their righteousness and justification stifles the intimate relationship with God because a believer feels "unworthy" to fellowship with Him.

Condemnation is a major obstacle that must be conquered in order to develop a deep, personal relationship with God. Condemnation is present when believers look down on themselves and try to become worthy enough to walk and talk with God by their own works. Either unintentionally or even intentionally they, as well as all people, feel that they have done something wrong.

For all have sinned, and come short of the glory of God (Romans 3:23).

This is why God sent Jesus Christ into the world as the payment for all sins. Thus He was the payment for sins committed before the new birth.

Whom God hath set forth to be a propitiation [payment] *through faith in His blood, to declare His*

6

righteousness for the remission of sins that are past, through the forbearance of God (Romans 3:25).

He is also the payment for sins committed after the new birth.

My little children, these things write I unto you, that ye sin not. And if any man sin, we have an advocate with the Father, Jesus Christ the righteous: and He is the propitiation [payment] *for our sins: and not for ours only, but also for the sins of the whole world* (1 John 2:1-2).

Because Jesus Christ is the payment for all sins and short-comings, there is therefore now no need for condemnation or self-justification (see Rom. 8:1).

Self-justification is focusing on one's own works more than on the grace of God. Christian believers are exhorted to be strong in the Lord and in the power of His might (see Eph. 6:10)—not their own might, works, or personal accomplishments.

Isn't it wonderful to know that God does not deal with us according to our own works and merit, but according to His grace?

The Lord is merciful and gracious, slow to anger, and plenteous in mercy. He will not always chide: neither will He keep His anger for ever. He hath not dealt with us after our sins; nor rewarded us according to our iniquities. For as the heaven is high above the earth, so great is His mercy toward them that fear Him. As far as the east is from the west, so far hath He removed our transgressions from us. Like as a father pitieth his children, so the Lord pitieth them that fear Him. For He knoweth our frame; He remembereth that we are dust (Psalm 103:8-14).

Instead of dwelling upon their own accomplishments, Christians need to remember and believe in what Jesus Christ accomplished for them.

And be found in Him [Christ], *not having mine own righteousness, which is of the law, but that which is through the faith of Christ, the righteousness which is of God by faith* (Philippians 3:9).

This is the spiritual vitality of the grace of God. God forgave us of all of our sins and shortcomings and made us righteous in His sight. We did not receive this by our works, but by having faith in Jesus Christ.

It is understandable from a human point of view that believers are overwhelmed by the goodness of God. They may even consider that this grace is "too good to be true." They know that they were once enemies of God, that they walked contrary to God's will, and even held God in contempt. However, the great delivering truth is that by the grace of God—through the sacrifice of Jesus Christ—believers have been made worthy to have this relationship with God.

This "holy ground" of standing in the grace of God is also bloody ground because Jesus Christ gave His life that all of His brethren could stand there with Him. It may not have cost us anything to gain it, but it cost Jesus Christ His life. This is why the "holy ground" of standing in the grace of God must be diligently guarded. Yes, this grace of God came to us as an unmerited gift, but Jesus Christ had to fight for it and win it for us. We should therefore rise with righteous indignation against the enemy and claim what our Lord accomplished for us.

The battle cry of "No More Condemnation!" should rumble out of God's throne room of grace as believers stand righteously before Him.

> *There is therefore now no condemnation to them which are in Christ Jesus, who walk not after the flesh, but after the Spirit. For the law of the Spirit of life in Christ Jesus hath made me free from the law of sin and death. For what the law could not do, in that it was weak through the flesh, God sending His own Son in the likeness of sinful flesh, and for sin, condemned sin in the flesh: that the righteousness of the law might be fulfilled in us, who walk not after the flesh, but after the Spirit* (Romans 8:1-4).

The righteousness of the law was fulfilled in Jesus Christ. To stand strong in the accomplishments of Jesus Christ is to stand strong in grace. What believers *do* holds little significance in light of what Jesus Christ *has done* to make them worthy to fellowship with God. Regardless of how anyone feels, "there is therefore now no condemnation to them which are in Christ Jesus."

> *Thou therefore, my son, be strong in the grace that is in Christ Jesus* (2 Timothy 2:1).

The words of another old hymn, "Unworthy," summarize the truth of grace when dealing with walking and talking with God:

But He made me worthy and now by His grace,
a son now I walk with my Lord.

Ask yourself:

Am I trying to develop a relationship with God based upon my works?

Is God's goodness and grace the foundation of my fellowship with God?

Remember: Be Strong in Grace.

Stay simple. Be strong in grace. Be humble. Stay your mind on God. Accept that He works within you. Ask God. He will teach you.

Chapter 2

Be Humble

The heart of the humble child of God diligently seeks for understanding of the voice of the Father. Could there be a pearl of more precious price than the recognition of the Father's voice? The humble child of God says, "Father, teach me to know when You speak. I want to know You. I want to walk and talk with You."

God is your Father, Teacher, and closest Friend. He will teach you to recognize His voice when you are humble. When the child of God humbly admits and says, "Father, I need Your help," God graciously gives more grace.

But He [God] *giveth more grace. Wherefore he saith, God resisteth the proud, but giveth grace unto the humble* (James 4:6).

Having humility is fundamental in learning when God speaks to you. This attitude shuns pride and admits the need for help. God does not resist ignorance, but He does resist the prideful attitude.

...and be clothed with humility: for God resisteth the proud, and giveth grace to the humble (1 Peter 5:5).

Being humble is a great lesson in life. Often being humble is thought to mean being weak, but in actuality, this attribute is the great strength of a Christian's life. All great men and women of God have had to learn this lesson. It is of great profit and is easily learned when the teacher is the God of all love, our heavenly Father.

One of the greatest verses of Scripture that defines humility and shows how God works with humble people is Isaiah 57:15.

For thus saith the high and lofty One that inhabiteth eternity, whose name is Holy; I [God] dwell in the high and holy place, with him also that is of a contrite and humble spirit, to revive the spirit of the humble, and to revive the heart of the contrite ones (Isaiah 57:15).

Being humble means "to be low." It does not mean to be low in self-esteem, or to be of less stature in the sight of other people, but low underneath God who is the high and lofty One. This means to be beneath God and in subjection to His will.

Even though being humble means to be underneath God, this is man's highest and most exalted place. This is where God intended for His people to dwell—under the wing of His loving protection and care. This is where intimate fellowship with God occurs because this is where man abides in harmony with God. Is this not what we are pursuing—to dwell with God? Do we not want to abide where intimate conversations with Him take place? This is God's promise to humble people.

Humility is the state of mind that accepts God as the high and lofty One. This comes from the understanding that God is omniscient and therefore smarter than all. Humility is the attitude that accepts that God is smarter than you and so is able to help you. Being humble before God is allowing Him to be the high and lofty One—in charge of all things. He gives the orders—we obey. He is the omniscient teacher and counsellor. In other words, He is the boss, director, foreman, manager, overseer, supervisor, and chief.

God exhorts His children to let Him be the one in charge. He resists the attitude of pride and gives more grace to the humble. He promises the humble ones that He will lift them up to high places when they humble themselves before Him.

Humble yourselves therefore under the mighty hand of God, that He may exalt you in due time (1 Peter 5:6).

Since God is the high and lofty One, the attitude of His humble children is to allow Him to be on the pedestal of honor. This is not a begrudging attitude that smugly accepts God's position and sullenly carries out His orders. On the contrary, this means to be tender in one's heart toward God and lovingly in subjection to Him.

Because thine heart was tender, and thou didst humble thyself before God, when thou heardest His words against this place, and against the inhabitants thereof, and humbledst thyself before Me, and didst rend thy clothes, and weep before Me; I have even heard thee also, saith the Lord (2 Chronicles 34:27).

True humility includes being tender in your heart before God. Putting Second Chronicles 34:27 and Psalm 10:17 together reveals a wonderful truth concerning walking and talking with God.

Lord, Thou hast heard the desire of the humble: Thou wilt prepare their heart, Thou wilt cause Thine ear to hear (Psalm 10:17).

The humble person prepares to hear God speaking by being tender in heart before Him. This is the preparation we are seeking. We want to be prepared to hear when God speaks. It comes from being tender in the innermost part of your soul to God.

Being tender in your heart and humble before God is to be primarily concerned with doing God's will instead of your own. This is summarized in the familiar saying, "Seek God first." To be self-centered causes the heart to be hardened with selfish ideas. This leads to people serving themselves before God.

As mentioned previously, the requirements to walk and talk with God are minimal, but a basic prerequisite is to be humble and tender in your heart before God. This tenderness in heart toward God is not a luxury for the child who wants to walk and talk with the Father; it is a necessity. Tenderness toward God is what He requires to effectively work within someone. Whether this attitude is seen by others is of little consequence, for God looks on the heart (see 1 Sam. 16:7).

The great men and women who have been showered with God's grace have been tender in their hearts before God. This presents an interesting question. When humble people receive more grace from God, does this mean that God shows favoritism toward them and is a respecter of persons?

The phrase "God is no respecter of persons" has been loosely used and seldom considered for its true meaning. This phrase means that God does not make something available to one person while denying the same thing to another. In the words of Matthew 5:45, God makes the rain fall on the just as well as on the unjust. However, when an individual chooses to perform those things that are well-pleasing in God's sight, God certainly does respect that person and even shows special favors of grace toward him. God most definitely has respect for anyone who is tender toward Him and does those things that are pleasing in His sight.

God is no respecter of persons because He makes all things available to everyone. However, when one accepts the position of God as being the high and holy One, and is tender in heart toward God and humble, he in turn obviously receives more grace.

This brings up another interesting point: people rarely consider God as a separate entity with His own desires. Does not God have a free will and the privilege of exercising it? Can He not choose the people with whom He desires to fellowship? Does He not have the prerogative of blessing those whom He chooses?

Furthermore, do people consider the fact that God could have a relationship with a particular person simply because He enjoys that particular person's company? Unfortunately, not recognizing these things hinders the development of the relationship.

God has revealed in His Word that He chooses to dwell with humble people who are tender in their hearts toward Him. When a believer discovers this from God's Word and consequently develops humility and tenderness, God notices, and the foundation for an intimate relationship is laid.

God would be a respecter of persons if He had not made this relationship available to everyone. Developing an intimate walking and talking relationship with God is not a second work of grace—it is properly using the first and only work of grace. Simply put: when an individual is humble before God, God chooses to "hang out" with that one.

Any person can choose to walk in God's ways and develop this relationship. Those people who are humble and consider God's will above their own have great grace in their lives. God gives more grace according to His own free will. This is why humble people enjoy great relationships with God.

Is this so different from you or me? Do you like arrogant people who constantly try to put themselves above you, or have you chosen friends who are loving, cordial, tender, and supportive?

When I first moved into the community where I now live, I met a fellow minister. From the first time we met, I found an unassuming, genuine man who loved God and me. When he discovered that I had a somewhat broad biblical background, he quickly disclosed his desire to have a greater knowledge of the Scriptures and directly asked me if I would help him. Not long after our initial meeting, I discovered that he needed some help with his church bulletin. I was more than glad to help him with biblical matters, but here was an opportunity to do more. I wanted to do even more because he was so loving and humble. We had become friends. Neither of us tried to "lord" our positions over the other. We wanted to be partners in the ministry of helping others and each other. I had found a humble man; I had found a friend.

Is it so foreign to think that God enjoys the company of people who like Him? Could it be that God, Himself, desires to develop relationships with people who are pure, unassuming, loving, kind, obedient, and humble?

There are many examples of such people in the Bible. Moses, David, Abraham, and Mary were people with whom God had special relationships. Moses knew God face to face; Abraham was a friend of God; David was a man after God's own heart; and Mary was the handmaiden of the Lord.

Does this mean that these individuals were "specially blessed"? No. It means that they were given the opportunity, just like all others, to develop a relationship with God. They faithfully seized the moment and did it. Furthermore, the fact that the Word of God records these special relationships, and since God is no respecter of persons, indicates that these relationships are available for us, too.

The question to be asked and the lesson to be learned is, "What did these people do that caused a special relationship with God to develop?" The answer is simple. They were humble. God likes humble people who are tender in their hearts before Him. Their hearts are prepared to walk and talk with God—to listen to God when He speaks.

Moses' humility and meekness earned him the distinction of knowing God face to face.

(Now the man Moses was very meek [humble], *above all the men which were upon the face of the earth)* (Numbers 12:3).

And there arose not a prophet since in Israel like unto Moses, whom the Lord knew face to face (Deuteronomy 34:10).

When God's Word says that a person "found grace in the sight of the Lord," it indicates that the person was humble and willing to do the will of God. Noah, Isaac, Jacob, Gideon, Job, Ruth, etc., were all such people. These were humble people with special walking and talking relationships with God. Abraham was such a man also.

And the scripture was fulfilled which saith, Abraham believed God, and it was imputed unto him for righteousness: and he was called the Friend of God (James 2:23).

To be called God's friend is a title of great distinction. Abraham was God's friend; God liked him. It was not because Abraham had lots of money or was born in a particular family. God enjoyed Abraham's company because Abraham was concerned about doing God's will more than his own. Abraham was humble. When God told him to get up and go, Abraham got up and went. He did not ask God to explain the whole trip and to draw a detailed map. He did not complain about the inconvenience of God's calling in his life; he simply obeyed. God liked Abraham; they were friends. God had a great relationship with Abraham and Moses. Similarly, David was humble, tender, and sought after God with his whole heart.

And when He had removed him [Saul], *He raised up unto them David to be their king; to whom also He gave testimony, and said, I have found David the son of Jesse, a man after Mine own heart, which shall fulfil all My will* (Acts 13:22).

David was a humble man. This is what is meant when the Word of God says that David was a man "after" God's own heart. Simply stated, David knew about God from His Word, but then he sought after God by fervently doing God's will. Psalm 63 tells of David's commitment to seek after God; it says in verse 8 that he followed "hard" after God. David sought "after" God's pleasure. By David's free will, his choice of humility, and his heart to obey God's Word, he gained the distinction of being "a man after God's own heart."

Another great example of humility is Mary, the mother of our Lord Jesus Christ. Notice the usages of "humility" and "exalt" in the following Scriptures. These indicate the kind of person whom God chose to bring His Son into the world and raise Him in the nurture and admonition of the Lord. Listen to what Mary said about the benefits of being humble as opposed to being proud.

And Mary said, My soul doth magnify the Lord, and my spirit hath rejoiced in God my Saviour. For He hath regarded the low estate [humility] *of His handmaiden: for, behold, from henceforth all generations shall call me blessed. ... He hath shewed strength with His arm; He hath scattered the proud in the imagination of their hearts. He hath put down the mighty from their seats, and exalted* [made high] *them of low degree* [of humility] (Luke 1:46-48,51-52).

God was able to work with Mary because she was humble. Mary was not concerned with thinking herself better than others; she wanted only to do the will of God and be humble in His sight. Mary knew that she literally could not bring forth spiritual fruit by her flesh. This is why Mary was chosen to be the mother of the Messiah; she was humble. God could work with her; she received "more" grace.

The single common trait that all these people shared is their humility. Humility is necessary to build a great relationship with God. Since God is no respecter of persons and had close relationships with these people, then likewise if you are humble, you can enjoy a close relationship with Him also.

Of all the relationships enjoyed through the ages, none can compare to the intimacy between God and His Son, Jesus Christ. Jesus Christ was the only begotten of the Father. When God brought Him into the world He said, "Let all the angels worship Him" (see Heb. 1:6). The angels announced Him as "Christ the Lord" (Lk. 2:11).

Yet even Jesus Christ, having the exalted position of the Son of God, knew who was the high and lofty Holy One. When one addressed Him as "Good Master," His reply was, "Why callest thou Me good? There is none good but God" (see Mt. 19:16-17). His sole purpose in life was to carry out His Father's business. His "meat" was to do the will of God who sent Him and to finish His work (see Jn. 4:34).

Then answered Jesus and said unto them, Verily, verily, I say unto you, The Son can do nothing of Himself, but what He seeth the Father do: for what things soever He doeth, these also doeth the Son likewise. For the Father loveth the Son, and sheweth Him all things that Himself doeth: and He will shew Him greater works than these, that ye may marvel (John 5:19-20).

Notice the humility of our Lord Jesus Christ—how He subjected Himself under the will of His Father. Observe the openness and intimacy that He had with His Father. Jesus Christ was satisfied to be subjected under the mighty hand of God. He even subjected Himself unto the horrible death of the cross.

But made Himself of no reputation, and took upon Him the form of a servant, and was made in the likeness of men: and being found in fashion as a man, He humbled Himself, and became obedient unto death, even the death of the cross. Wherefore God also hath highly exalted Him, and given Him a name which is above every name: that at the name of Jesus every knee should bow, of things in heaven, and things in earth, and things under the earth; and that every tongue should confess that Jesus Christ is Lord, to the glory of God the Father (Philippians 2:7-11).

Of all the men and women who ever lived, Jesus Christ was the most humble. He was the most humble and also the most exalted. It is Jesus who is seated at the most prominent and exalted place—the right hand of God.

The lesson that humility teaches us is great. We have the examples of Moses, Abraham, David, Mary, and especially the Lord Jesus Christ. God does not dwell with the arrogant or proud, but with the humble. It is to them that He gives more grace.

> *But He giveth more grace. Wherefore he saith, God resisteth the proud, but giveth grace unto the humble* (James 4:6).

You can receive more grace and enjoy an intimate walking and talking relationship with God when you are humble. You can dwell in lofty places with Him and enjoy His company when you are tender in your heart before Him.

> *For thus saith the high and lofty One that inhabiteth eternity, whose name is Holy; I dwell in the high and holy place, with him also that is of a contrite and humble spirit, to revive the spirit of the humble, and to revive the heart of the contrite ones* (Isaiah 57:15).

Humble ones seek after God's will; they seek Him with their whole heart. Their hearts are prepared with tenderness to hear from Him. The humble ones seek God's counsel. They acknowledge Him in all their ways; they allow Him to direct their steps. When they hear from God, they obey. They ask God how to do what He wants done. They wait for His answer. They know God as the living, vital reality of love who calls Himself "Father."

God knows if you recognize His voice when He speaks to you. He also knows if you do not recognize Him when He speaks. A humble response to this is, "Father, teach me. Even if I know a little, teach me more. The greatest treasure in my life is to walk and talk with You. I am Your child. I am humble; teach me."

God is your Father. He is also your Teacher. Ask Him how to recognize His voice. He will teach you.

The second strand in the "braid of simplicity" is "be humble." It is interwoven into the strand of grace. God gives more grace to the humble.

Ask yourself:

Do I honestly know when God speaks to me?

Have I personally asked God to help me understand when He does? If not, why not do so now.

Remember: Be Humble

Stay simple. Be strong in grace. Be humble. Stay your mind on God. Accept that He works within you. Ask God. He will teach you.

Chapter 3

Stay Your Mind on God

To recognize when God speaks to you, you must be strong in grace, be humble, and have your mind stayed upon Him to hear when He speaks.

The "stayed mind" is similar to keeping your radio tuned to the proper frequency, so you can hear when God speaks.

Thou wilt keep him in perfect peace, whose mind is stayed on Thee: because he trusteth in Thee (Isaiah 26:3).

God gives perfect peace when the mind is stayed on Him. This keeps the mind in order and keeps it from wandering. The stayed mind is where the energized thoughts of God are most easily distinguished from your own thoughts.

The "stayed mind" is the fixed, focused, and disciplined mind. It is a wonderful attribute and is worthy of developing, but even more fundamental than wanting a stayed mind is the question, "*Why* is one wanted?"

The Word of God reveals that there is a duty to discipline the thinking, but is the duty in response to God's calling or to wanting success in other endeavors? Since the whole duty of mankind is to love the Lord God with all the heart, soul, and *mind* (Mt. 22:37), the motive for staying the mind should be to love God and have fellowship with Him.

Within the arena of walking and talking with God, the stayed mind is a necessity. It is keeping the mind fixed on God, enabling believers to recognize when the still, small voice from God is energized.

Be still, and know that I am God (Psalm 46:10a).

Perhaps many Christians have heard of the "still, small voice." This is the reference to the energized thoughts that come into the conscious awareness of believers when God works within them. This still, small voice was heard by Elijah. He was in the midst of a storm, earthquake, and fire. He had been pursued by King Ahab and had his life threatened by Jezebel. He had gone into the mountains to hide and preserve his life. In the midst of the tumult and fear for his life, Elijah got quiet. He got still in his mind. He stayed his mind on God so that he was peaceful enough to hear from Him.

And he came thither unto a cave, and lodged there; and, behold, the word of the Lord came to him, and He said unto him, What doest thou here, Elijah? And he said, I have been very jealous for the Lord God of hosts: for the children of Israel have forsaken thy covenant, thrown down thine altars, and slain thy prophets with the sword; and I, even I only, am left; and they seek my life, to take it away. And He said, Go forth, and stand upon the mount before the Lord. And, behold, the Lord passed by, and a great and strong wind rent the mountains, and brake in pieces the rocks before the Lord; but the Lord was not in the wind: and after the wind an earthquake; but the Lord was not in the earthquake: and after the earthquake a fire; but the Lord was not in the fire: and after the fire a still small voice (1 Kings 19:9-12).

This is a great lesson and practical instruction for every Christian. When the turmoil, chaos, and confusion of the world threatens your sanity and peace, the storms are never so great that you cannot hear from God. The adversary huffs and puffs and tries to blow away your fellowship with God. You may not always be able to retreat to the mountains as Elijah did, but you can always stay your mind on God and allow Him to give you the perfect peace that you need in order to hear from Him.

Thou [God] *wilt keep him in perfect peace, whose mind is stayed on Thee: because he trusteth in Thee* (Isaiah 26:3).

The peace that comes from the stayed mind returns to simplicity. Peace is the absence of confusion. This is what allows one to recognize the voice of God, not only while in prayer and when questions are asked, but also in the midst of everyday activities. When believers are strong in grace, humble, and accept that God is working within them, then, the stayed mind will allow them to recognize the still, small voice of God being energized within them at any time.

The only individual who ever walked perfectly was, not coincidentally, the same one who perfectly exhibited the stayed mind. Jesus Christ always maintained His focus on God. His stayed mind and perfect peace enabled Him to always recognize the voice and instruction from His Father.

Jesus Christ met the onslaught and deception of the adversary face-to-face. With a mind stayed on God, He properly responded with, "It is written... ." He was caught in angry seas, interrogated by lecherous Pharisees, and faced accusative devil spirits, but He always controlled His mind and kept it stayed on God. This mental stability allowed our Lord and perfect example to always recognize when God energized thoughts into His conscious awareness. He always obeyed God, but before He could obey the Father's will, He had to know when God spoke to Him. Only then could He carry it out.

To stay the mind, it is necessary to understand from a biblical perspective how the mind works. This is important in being able to sort and distinguish between thoughts that God energizes into the mind and thoughts that come from other sources.

The Realm and Function of the Mind

The following statement is fundamental to understanding *how* to control your mind. **Your mind is only an organ of perception. It is your thinking apparatus. Your mind is not you; it is only a part of you.**

One reason people have had difficulty in controlling the mind is that they do not realize the mind is only part of them and is a controllable organ. The mind, like the heart, lungs, or eyes is a functioning organ. The functions of organs within the body are described by two words: involuntary and voluntary. Involuntary organs do not have to be told to work. Voluntary ones have to be told to function. In other words, upon arising from sleep, the heart, an involuntary organ, does not have to be commanded to "beat"; the feet, however, which are voluntary, must be told to "hit the floor."

The mind is both involuntary and voluntary. It is involuntary only because it operates without being told to, but it is voluntary because you can tell it what to do.

Statements such as "make up your mind," or "change your mind," indicate that the mind is controllable and therefore has a voluntary function. Since the mind is the thinking apparatus, it is not a person in totality. It is the organ that allows the person to think and therefore to make decisions.

The mind has three basic functions. It gathers information, stores information, and gives back the information. Since our concern is in distinguishing between information that is received, the aspect of receiving information is our primary concern.

The mind of a Christian believer can receive information from several sources. It can receive information from the physical body, from the senses' input outside of the body, or from the spirit of God within. To the mind, the pain of a splinter in the finger, the score of the World Series, or spiritual foreknowledge of economic events are all just pieces of information to be processed.

Christians have a source of information that non-Christians do not have. The non-Christian, or natural man, does not have the holy spirit and therefore is limited by the information he can receive. He is limited to what is received from either his physical body or his senses' input from the surrounding world. A body-and-soul man can therefore only deduce natural conclusions. He does not have the "problem" of sorting natural thoughts from spiritual thoughts.

> *But the natural man* [of body and soul] *receiveth not the things of the Spirit of God: for they are foolishness unto him: neither can he know them, because they are spiritually discerned* (1 Corinthians 2:14).

A Christian believer, however, has body, soul, and spirit. He may receive natural or spiritual information. Therefore, spirit-filled people may derive either natural or spiritual conclusions. Although the natural man may not have the dilemma of sorting between natural or spiritual thoughts, he will never have the joy and benefits of fellowship with God, nor the possibility of receiving information beyond five-senses reasoning.

The mind, being simply the organ of mental perception, is not affected by the new birth of the holy spirit, except that it now has another portal from which information arrives.

The mind is only an organ and is not responsible for distinguishing between natural and spiritual thoughts. Its job is to receive the information and deliver it to your conscious awareness. Your responsibility is to determine the source of the information and to decide whether the thought is natural or spiritual. To recognize spiritually energized thoughts from God, each thought must be seized and sorted. The mind must therefore be controlled.

Controlling the Mind

Controlling the mind is similar to driving a car. There are only two types of controls—speed and direction. Some cars, like some minds, have the capacity to go faster than others, but how fast the car goes is of little consequence if it arrives at the wrong destination or wrecks before arriving.

To arrive at a predetermined destination, the speed of the mind must be controlled to handle one thought at a time. Controlling each thought is the primary consideration of the stayed mind when distinguishing the difference between natural and spiritual thoughts.

> *Casting down imaginations, and every high thing that exalteth itself against the knowledge of God, and bringing into captivity every* [each] *thought to the obedience of Christ* (2 Corinthians 10:5).

This verse seems massively challenging when believers look at capturing all thoughts of the mind at once. However, it is not overwhelming to control one thought at a time. This is the exhortation of this verse. (The Greek translation is to lead captive "each" thought to the obedience of Christ.)

Before a thought can be brought into obedience, it must be captured. Notice that Second Corinthians 10:5 does not say to bring all thoughts into captivity. Though capturing all thoughts is the ultimate desire, all thoughts may be captured only by seizing them one at time.

Speed Control

To capture each thought, the speed of the mind must be controlled to handle them one at a time. This introduces the control of the mind that must first be handled—speed. Not knowing that the mind has a speed control has caused believers to be confused, make wrong decisions, and have many sleepless nights.

Controlling the speed of the mind is a prerequisite to controlling the direction. Are there not speed limits in Driver's Education classes? The goal of controlling the speed of the mind is not to go slowly, but to go as quickly as possible while still being able to bring each thought into captivity. The primary goal in walking with God is not necessarily to walk quickly, but correctly. Is this not the exhortation of "Be still, and know that I am God"? (See Psalm 46:10a.)

In order to lead a thought captive to the obedience of Christ, the thought must be captured and weighed according to the standard of the Word of God. There are variables that determine how quickly thoughts can come, such as physical ability, nutrition, rest, attitude, etc., but knowledge of the Word of God must always be the standard of how quickly one allows his mind to run. This is the exhortation in First Corinthians 2:13.

Which things also we speak, not in the words which man's wisdom teacheth, but which the Holy Ghost teacheth; comparing spiritual things with spiritual (1 Corinthians 2:13).

Spiritually-received thoughts must be compared to the spiritual words of the Word of God. The main goal in controlling the speed of the mind is to match the arrival speed of thoughts with the knowledge of Scripture so the energized thoughts of God may be recognized. Consequently, most believers need to hear the following exhortation: *Slow down!*

The fast pace of society is an enemy of godliness and sound spiritual thinking. The constant barrage of fiery darts (in the form of ungodly thoughts and images) is sent by the adversary to distract and "overload" the mind of a believer. The adversary's aim is to prevent the believer from having a peaceful and simple fellowship with God. The adversary may control the speed of society, but he does not have control over the speed of your mind.

It is inconceivable that anyone would want to think quickly at the expense of thinking correctly. This could only happen because the accepted way of thinking has been programmed by someone (the adversary) who wants confusion and turmoil to flourish. The adversary is pushing "go fast" while the true God advocates peace, order, and control of one's mind.

The adversary's goal is to destroy fellowship between God and His children. He has no success in distracting God so he works on God's kids. Do not get caught in this game. If it is necessary to slow down the speed of your mind to match your knowledge of Scripture, at least you will arrive at the proper destination.

Adversarial thoughts may tell you that you will get behind in the world by learning to slow down in your thinking. Ask yourself, "Will it be better for me to be at the wrong place even if I am early?"

When thoughts arrive more quickly than your available knowledge of Scripture can sort them, confusion results. A bottleneck of confusion will gather and thoughts from God will "slip by undetected." Have you ever said in retrospect, "God told me to do that. I just did not realize it was God who told me"? If so, you were going too fast.

You can go faster as your knowledge of Scripture increases. Always keep your hand on the throttle of your mind and do not allow it to go faster than you can control. Do not allow thoughts to "slip by" and not be led captive to the obedience of Christ.

A friend of mine said to me once, "You say that God will always direct your path." (Actually, I did not say it. I quoted it from Proverbs 3:6.) He said, "Why is it that when I come to an intersection, and ask God which way to go, I do not hear anything?" I quietly asked Father what to tell him. Father said, "Tell him that you know but that you are not going to tell him." That is what I did. A couple of months later, he asked me again. This time Father told me that I could tell him and I began to realize why I needed to wait to give him an explanation.

"First," I said, "if I had told you the answer a couple of months ago, you would not have appreciated it or even remembered it. The reason that I did not tell you when you asked is the same reason that you do not hear from God when you ask Him questions. You are in such a hurry that you are more concerned in getting where you want to go than you are about talking and fellowshiping with your heavenly Father." I also told him, "If it is important enough to ask God, then take the time to wait for an answer. *Slow down!*"

When the adversary invented the problem of "speed thinking," he also marketed the solutions of drugs, alcohol, and "downers" to sedate the mind. This has become recreation for many people. Some call this "stress relief." Stress exists because the adversary accelerates the speed of society and believers ignorantly try to keep pace.

Isaiah 26:3 says that perfect peace is given by God when the mind is stayed on Him, but the world says you can have peace when you have absence of stress. People will never achieve absence of stress if they do not personally put their hands on the speed control of their own minds and stay their minds on God. Controlling the speed of the mind requires constant vigilance. This may be difficult for people because there has been a lack of teaching regarding it; furthermore, the pressures of the world keep trying to force believers to keep pace with it.

Never allow the speed of your mind to go faster than you can control. Ask yourself, "Will I be better off to arrive at the right place a little later, or to arrive at the wrong place on time?" Hurry causes stress. Stress causes confusion. Confusion causes the energized thoughts from God to slip by along with the other thoughts "flying" through the mind. The energized thoughts of God can then be camouflaged with confusion.

When God speaks to you in the quietness of your heart and mind, have the speed of your mind controlled so you hear and recognize His voice. If necessary, slow down and match the speed of your mind with your knowledge of the Scriptures so you can lead captive every thought to the obedience of Christ.

One effective way to learn how to control the speed of your mind is to take time to be alone with God. Consciously, and even verbally, talk things over with Him. This is not an escape from people or problems, but is your personal time to be with God and develop your relationship with Him. Do not allow the adversary, working through the fast pace and pressure of society, to tell you that you are too busy to spend time with God.

Spending time alone with God will help you to learn how to discipline your mind in acknowledging God in everything you do.

In all thy ways acknowledge Him, and He shall direct thy paths (Proverbs 3:6).

Acknowledging God is called several things. Most simply it is called prayer. It is also called practicing the presence of God. Whatever it is called, the meaning is the same. Everything that you do—do it with Him. God is in you and with you in every situation. He is your Father, Teacher, constant Companion, and Friend. In all your ways, acknowledge His presence.

It is usually thought that prayer means asking God for His blessing and supply. Although this is certainly a great part of prayer, another important emphasis includes the simple communication with Him and the recognition that God is present and available to help. Thus prayer is the most dynamic force in the Christian life. If fellowship with God is thought of as a tree, then the roots are prayer. Pray about everything. Ask God for His counsel. Through prayer develop the consciousness of being "God-inside-minded" and acknowledge Him in everything you do.

Prayer will help you control the speed of your mind to detect when God energizes His thoughts into your conscious awareness.

Many people believe that the ministry of Jesus Christ lasted less than a year. Others think that it lasted three years. No matter how long it lasted, Jesus Christ was in the wilderness for the first 40 days of His ministry. Immediately after receiving the full measure of the spirit from God, He was in the wilderness for 40 days. If He invested those first 40 days of His precious time on earth in seeking God, then perhaps it would serve everyone desiring to walk like Him to also spend time with God.

Remember to match the speed of your mind with the knowledge of Scripture that you have. Once you have controlled the speed to handle one thought at a time, controlling the direction will be much easier.

Direction Control

Controlling the direction of the mind is a simple process. *You* tell it where to go. The mind is an involuntary organ because it runs without being told to operate, but it is primarily a voluntary organ because it can be controlled and directed where to go.

The mind should be directed toward "seeking after the things of God."

But seek ye first the kingdom of God, and His righteousness; and all these things shall be added unto you (Matthew 6:33).

To control direction, a fixed point must be headed toward and not veered away from. For the child of God, the fixed point of orientation for directing the mind is toward *God.*

But if from thence thou shalt seek the Lord thy God, thou shalt find Him, if thou seek Him with all thy heart and with all thy soul (Deuteronomy 4:29).

The mind needs to be directed positively toward godly subjects. In order to have the proper directional control for the mind, it needs to be told specifically where to go. It is a voluntary organ and needs to be directed.

The phrase "a wandering mind" means the directional controls have been released. When released to wander involuntarily, the mind usually goes toward the senses' realm. According to Ephesians 2:2-3, the natural tendency of the mind is to go to the lust of the flesh and of the mind. The mind will stop wandering when it is directed where to go. To get the mind directed away from the things of the flesh, send it to "spiritual things."

> *For they that are after the flesh do mind the things of the flesh; but they that are after the Spirit* [do mind] *the things of the Spirit* (Romans 8:5).

Too often people try to control the direction of the mind by telling it where *not* to go. This is called "not-not thinking." The mind does not respond to commands of where *not* to go. If you tell your mind to not go to the things of the flesh, it will look for the place it is not supposed to go—the flesh. For example, if you tell it to not think about apples, it will think about not thinking about apples and therefore recall details about apples. This "not-not thinking" is exhausting and counterproductive. To get your mind to "not" think about apples, for example, tell it to think about oranges.

The proper direction and place to send the mind to not think about things of the flesh is to send it to "do the will of God."

Philippians 2:13 and Second Corinthians 10:5 are foundational truths in this study. The verses following each of these are "directional commands." Each verse tells you to direct your mind toward obeying and doing the will God.

Do all things without murmurings and disputings
(Philippians 2:14).

"Do it!"

*And having in a readiness to revenge all disobedience,
when your obedience is fulfilled* (2 Corinthians 10:6).

"Obey!"

Is not the most important reason for wanting a walking, talking relationship with God so that you can know Him and His will? The purpose for wanting to know the will of God must be to do the will of God. The proper direction for sending the mind, therefore, is not only to "hear His voice," but especially to do what He says—to "obey His voice."

God may even command obedience, but ultimately, the mind of man must receive the commandment from God and direct his own will. The will of man is directed by his own decision. The mind may give alternatives and choices, but in the end, decisions are not made by the mind, but by the individual. The consummate choice made by man, by his own will, should be to do the will of God.

The will of God must be known from the Scriptures. Knowing the Scriptures is the only way the true direction of the mind can be determined. Reading, studying, and even memorizing sections of the Bible is not a luxury when endeavoring to recognize when God speaks to you. (In Chapter 4 we will discuss how one of the ways God speaks to you is by inspiring you to remember what He has told you in His Word.)

Many people have thought that spending time with God, whether in prayer or reading the Bible, means disciplining yourself. Instead of considering it as discipline, just delight yourself in God.

I delight to do Thy will, O my God: yea, Thy law is within my heart (Psalm 40:8).

Although developing the stayed mind takes work and commitment, the same result may be achieved by simply *delighting* yourself in the matter at hand. Then you will *want* to keep your mind stayed there because it is your desire and delight.

For example, most kids do not have to work diligently to develop a stayed mind on baseball. It is their *delight*. This is similar to the old saying, "The only difference between work and play is your attitude."

Often when you hear the statement, "Stay your mind on God," the emphasis is on *you* staying *your* mind. There is more emphasis placed on the necessity of discipline than there is on delighting yourself in the matter at hand.

If kids are told to stay their minds on baseball, the desire to play baseball would quickly fade. Likewise, when staying your mind on God, the more desired approach is to say, "Delight yourself in God."

Delight thyself also in the Lord; and He shall give thee the desires of thine heart (Psalm 37:4).

God will give you perfect peace when your mind is stayed on Him. The peaceful mind is where thoughts are most easily sorted. The peaceful organ of perception is where the voice and thoughts of God are most easily recognized. The stayed mind on God is where perfect peace is received. These are the benefits of delighting yourself in the Lord.

Another way to stay your mind upon God is to make His thoughts your thoughts through His Word.

For My thoughts are not your thoughts, neither are your ways My ways, saith the Lord. For as the heavens are higher than the earth, so are My ways higher than your ways, and My thoughts than your thoughts (Isaiah 55:8-9).

God's thoughts are revealed in His Word. When His thoughts and His ways are received and retained in the mind, the mind is stayed upon Him. This is the same as letting the Word of Christ dwell richly in you.

Let the word of Christ dwell in you richly in all wisdom; teaching and admonishing one another in psalms and hymns and spiritual songs, singing with grace in your hearts to the Lord (Colossians 3:16).

Being delighted in God is the great key to staying your mind upon Him. This can be done by staying in the posture of prayer and by allowing His Word to be the light of your life.

The stayed mind on God may be called many things. Call it a stayed mind; call it the controlled mind; call it the peaceful mind; call it practicing the presence of God; call it acknowledging God in everything—or simply call it prayer. Whatever it is called, it is to have the mental focus on God. All these things are summed up by simply saying,"Delight yourself in God." If you want to clearly hear God's voice, delight yourself in Him. This will keep you focused on Him and expecting to hear from Him.

Delight yourself in God.

In summary, both spiritual and natural thoughts come into the mind. Thoughts from the senses' realm as well as energized thoughts from God come into the same organ of perception. The mind must be controlled according to speed to sort the origin of these thoughts. Once the origin has been determined, the voice and commandments of God may be distinguished from the thoughts of the natural realm.

After the voice and commandment of God have been determined, then the decision to obey God can be made and the mind can be directed in that path. After God's will has been discovered, then the end may be accomplished: to do His will and good pleasure.

When the speed and direction of the mind are controlled, the mind can then be stayed. It is the stayed mind on God that gives the peace necessary to be able to consistently detect His energizing within us.

You Don't Have to Be Smart to Walk With God—simply stay your mind on Him.

Ask yourself:

Am I tuned to the right radio frequency for hearing God speak?

Is controlling my mind difficult?

Is the stayed mind discipline, or is God my true delight?

How much am I reading the Bible?

When I read the Bible, am I having fellowship with God?

Am I trying to think quickly at the expense of thinking correctly?

Am I thinking about what I am thinking about?

Remember: Stay Your Mind on God.

Stay simple. Be strong in grace. Be humble. Stay your mind on God. Accept that He works within you. Ask God. He will teach you.

Chapter 4

Accept That God Works Within You

This chapter contains the "meat" of the study. Here we will cover the vital aspect of understanding when God speaks to you. We will also study how to distinguish between God's voice and your own mind.

The previous chapters, "Be Strong in Grace," "Be Humble," and "Stay Your Mind on God" may seem less significant compared to this chapter. Nonetheless, the process of braiding strands together indicates that all aspects must be handled. This chapter is exciting, but it must be applied and understood in relation to the other aspects of walking with God in order to achieve its fullest understanding. To achieve the simple walk with God, the strands of grace, humility, and the stayed mind need to be woven together with this principle: "Accept that God works within you."

Walking and talking with God is available only because of God's faithfulness to perform Philippians 2:13.

For it is God which worketh in you both to will and to do of His good pleasure (Philippians 2:13).

God is at work within you.

The little word *is* is often taken for granted. "Is" is a present-tense, state-of-being verb. With this in mind, Philippians 2:13 becomes a foundation for those desiring to walk and talk with God. This verse states that God presently *is* working in you.

There is a tremendous difference between working to get something and working to recognize something that you already have. For example, there is a difference between working to get a car and learning how to drive a car you already have.

Philippians 2:13 is God's Word. *God* says that you do not have to work to receive this reality. It *is* already happening within you. Sometimes what a verse does not say speaks almost as loudly as what it does say. This verse does not say that God will work within you in the future, even though He will. It also does not say that He has worked within you in the past, even though He has. It says that God is at work within you presently.

In order for God to work within you, He needs to be already in you. He is in you by way of the presence of the gift of the holy spirit. The gift of the holy spirit was received when Romans 10:9 was confessed and believed.

That if thou shalt confess with thy mouth the Lord Jesus, and shalt believe in thine heart that God hath raised Him from the dead, thou shalt be saved (Romans 10:9).

At the time of salvation, the spirit of God in Christ in you, the holy spirit, was received. This gift is holy-pure, and it is spirit-life. This gift of pure spirit-life from God was created in your body and soul. Something exists within you that was never there before. That "something" is the holy-life of God. The promise of Philippians 2:13 is that the spirit of God which is already in you *is now* being energized within you. *When* God is working in you is what we are endeavoring to recognize.

Now concerning spiritual gifts [matters], *brethren, I would not have you ignorant* [without experiential knowledge]. *Ye know that ye were Gentiles, carried away unto these dumb* [silent] *idols, even as ye were led* (1 Corinthians 12:1-2).

God does not want us ignorant of spiritual matters. It is an important spiritual matter for you to understand when God is talking to you. God is the exact opposite of silent idols. He is alive and very talkative. He wants His children to listen to Him.

For it is God which worketh in you both to will and to do of His good pleasure (Philippians 2:13).

Since this verse holds such great truths, it should be examined for its inherent beauty and accuracy. The Greek word for "worketh" is *energon*. This word translates into the English language directly as "energizing." If something is being energized, a greater reality is energizing it. What is being energized within you is the gift of the holy spirit, but God is doing the energizing.

Grammatically, "worketh in" is a present participle. Therefore, to be more accurate this verse should read, "For it is God who is energizing in you." This means exactly what it says. God is presently and actively energizing in you. He is energizing thoughts and His good pleasure by way of the holy spirit into your mind.

To restate a fundamental truth, Philippians 2:13 needs only to be accepted. You do not need to do additional works to make you worthy to receive this or to "believe for" this reality. It is already happening. God is providing the energizing; you need to provide the acceptance and recognition. Too many have been taught that they may not be worthy to receive this gracious action from God. This insinuation is very subtle and causes feelings of inadequacy or incompetence in having a walking and talking relationship with God. Anyone who says that you must do extra things for God to work within you does not understand the present participle in Philippians 2:13.

Now, *how* to accept Philippians 2:13 into practical application is simple. Repeat this verse over and over again in your mind until you accept it as a reality. Say, "*God* is working in me, God *is* working in me, God is *working* in me, God is working *in* me, God is working in *me*."

This is a simple action that will yield dynamic spiritual results. How often the verse needs to be repeated depends upon how many times you need to accept it as a reality. Until you claim this truth as a reality in your life, the effectual working of the spirit of God within you will be greatly limited. Yet, because of God's grace and mercy, even if this truth is not fully accepted, God will still work within you. However, the joy of understanding His voice and the fullness of His fellowship will not be entirely realized.

Common Problems That Prevent Believers From Accepting That God Works Within Them

There are two basic problems that plague believers endeavoring to accept that God is working in them: sin-consciousness and self-consciousness. In both cases, the problem comes from taking the focus off God and placing it upon one's self. Both problems will be manifested by the feeling of unworthiness or inadequacy. This is why we are to be strong in grace. The solution to both of these problems is to focus on God's goodness, grace, and power and not on the weakness and inability of self.

Another major problem believers have is understanding that they are children of God and not servants. In Old Testament times, men and women who had the spirit from God and walked with Him operated somewhat differently than New Testament sons and daughters of God. Although some Old Testament believers had the spirit from God, they were servants of God and not sons. The spirit that the servants had was sufficient only to do their jobs. In New Testament times, men and women still serve, but they are children of God. The holy spirit within believers at this present time is not primarily for service, but for fellowship with their Father.

And because ye are sons, God hath sent forth the Spirit of His Son into your hearts, crying, Abba, Father (Galatians 4:6).

This explanation is offered to clear up a common misconception in many Christians' minds. In Old Testament times, there are records of phenomenal communication. This is how God had to work with His servants because of the spirit they had. The spirit that servants had was not a full measure of the spirit that sons of God enjoy, but rather a portion of the full measure of the spirit. (See Second Kings 2:9.)

For He [the Son] *whom God hath sent speaketh the words of God: for God giveth not the Spirit by measure unto Him* (John 3:34).

Sons of God do not have a portion of holy spirit measured out to them; they receive the full measure of the sonship spirit. God gave Jesus Christ and all of His children the full measure because they are sons of God, not just servants.

Because servants did not have the full measure of the spirit, God often had to "jolt" them into hearing His voice. This explains why God had to speak to them in phenomenal communication in many instances. This is not necessarily true with *sons* of God. God still has all of these means available to Him to communicate with His children, but He works within His children to speak quietly and tenderly as a Father through the full measure of the holy spirit.

If New Testament sons of God are waiting for dreams and visions to believe that God is working within them, they need to have this misconception cleared up. Although the same ways of Old Testament communication are presently available, God can work within His children with much more simplicity and quietness. He energizes the spirit within the believer, and the spirit brings His voice to the conscious awareness of that son or daughter. God does not need to "jolt" them because they have the full measure of the holy spirit within. Do not get caught in the trap of thinking that God is only working in you when you see visual revelation or hear an audible voice!

In this administration of sonship, God desires that His children fellowship with Him, not just do works of service for Him. Service for God is a wonderful response that children have as a result of God's goodness, but it is not the basis of their relationship with God. Do not think that God only works within you when you are doing works for Him. Expect the inner quiet voice from God as your loving Father rather than as your boss.

The guarantee of Holy Scripture is that God *is* energizing within you. As you accept that He *is* working within you and talking to you, the next consideration is to recognize the voice of God within you when He speaks.

The Voice of God Within You

What is being sought is very simple: It is to recognize when God spiritually energizes words and thoughts into your mind.

It is important to note that we are not dealing with God speaking in an audible voice heard "outside" of the mind. An illustration of this voice is in Matthew 3:16-17.

And Jesus, when He was baptized, went up straightway out of the water: and, lo, the heavens were opened unto Him, and He saw the Spirit of God descending like a dove, and lighting upon Him: and lo a voice from heaven, saying, This is My beloved Son, in whom I am well pleased (Matthew 3:16-17).

This voice was not in Jesus Christ; it was outside of His mind. Others heard it also. God, being God, can manifest Himself in the way He chooses. There are other recorded instances of an audible voice in the life and ministry of Jesus Christ (see Mt. 17:5; Jn. 12:28). There are also recorded instances of God speaking to people outside of energizing the spirit within them. For example, He spoke to Adam and Eve after the original sin (see Gen. 3:9); He appeared and spoke to Abraham when he was 99 years old (see Gen 17:1); and He spoke to Moses out of the burning bush (see Ex. 3:4). When God chooses to speak in an audible voice outside of the mind of the person hearing it, there is no problem hearing it or distinguishing who is speaking. The audible, outside voice is in the category of phenomenon—something beyond what God has promised in the Scriptures. Many occurrences of this are in the Bible. Perhaps it has happened to you. It is not guaranteed that God will speak to you in an *outside*, audible, phenomenal voice, but it is guaranteed by Philippians 2:13 that He is speaking to you on the *inside.*

We are dealing with understanding the voice of God as He energizes within you. How God talks to you is very simple. He energizes the spirit within you. What He says and how He says it is also simple. God reminds you of things that you already know or He teaches you things that you do not know.

What did Jesus say about this?

But the Comforter, which is the Holy Ghost, whom the Father will send in My name, He shall teach you all things, and bring all things to your remembrance, whatsoever I have said unto you (John 14:26).

When God energizes a thought within you, it will either be a reminder of something that you already know or will be something that you did not know before. When the message is a reminder, it is inspiration. When the message is something that you did not know before, it is revelation.

God Reminds You—Inspiration

The statement "bring all things to your remembrance" in John 14:26 holds great depth of understanding concerning God talking to you. To bring something to remembrance is simply to "re-mind." It is to have something brought back to your conscious awareness. The literal biblical definition of "to remind" is "to have something brought to the top of the mind." The Greek word for "remembrance" in John 14:26 is *hupomnesis*. *Hupo* means "under," and *mnesis* means "mind." To be reminded of something is to have it brought to the top of your mind. The Latin equivalent for *hupomnesis* is *suggestre*. Being reminded by God comes as a "suggestion."

An accurate word describing God's reminding is *inspiration*. Inspiration (in a spiritual sense) is being reminded by God. The breakdown of the word is "in-spirit-action," or the spirit in you in action. This is how the inspirational manifestations of interpretation of tongues and the manifestation of prophecy are operated. It is also how God brings information back to your remembrance in everyday living. He energizes the spirit of God within you to bring words to your mind that you have already learned and retained.

God may also remind you to get your car keys or that He loves you, or He may remind you of Philippians 2:13. He energizes the spirit of God within you; then the spirit brings to the top of your mind the desired information that is stored and retained in your mind. This reminding is not a loud, boisterous thought. It is a quiet suggestion that comes by the energized will of God.

It is obvious that things can be remembered without God causing it. For example, a song or a poem could remind you of a person or event in your past, or someone could remind you to pick up the laundry. Unbelievers who do not have a spiritual connection with God obviously remember things. Someone or something may say or do something that causes an association with a previously held thought. Then the remembrance would come to the top of the awareness in the mind. This remembering is by an association. The association may be a red string tied around the finger or a subtle suggestion by someone else. Regardless of whether the remembrance comes from an association or a reminder from someone else, this kind of recall comes from human origins.

When God assists in recalling, He energizes the gift of the holy spirit and the spirit energizes the thought to be brought to the top of the mind. It will come as a suggestion or a simple quiet thought. This kind of remembrance comes by the will of God and is inspiration (in-spirit-action.)

An example of this is seen in the Book of Acts. Peter had been to the household of Cornelius. (This was the first occurrence of Gentiles being added to the Church.) After Peter had spoken the Word of God to the Gentiles and they had received salvation, he started to baptize them with water. Just as he was about to do it...

*Then remembered I the word of the Lord, how that He
said, John indeed baptized with water; but ye shall be
baptized with the Holy Ghost* (Acts 11:16).

This remembrance was recalled by the spirit of God
within Peter. God simply reminded him what the Lord Jesus
Christ had said (which was recorded in Acts 1:5)—that John
baptized with water, but they were to be baptized with the
holy spirit. God energized the spirit of Christ in Peter to
bring back to his awareness the information he had previously heard.

This method of reminding is not only used by God to recall Scriptures and truths that He has previously shown you,
but this inspirational way of God working within you is also
where the great joy of companionship exists. The words of
God retained in the mind are brought to remembrance by
God. He reminds you of His love for you. He reminds you
that He will never leave you nor forsake you. Inspirational
talks of love, encouragement, peace, and comfort come from
God bringing thoughts to your remembrance. You talk; He
listens. He reminds; you listen. This is a great aspect of fellowship with God.

*But the Comforter, which is the Holy Ghost, whom the
Father will send in My name, He shall teach you all
things, and bring all things to your remembrance,
whatsoever I have said unto you* (John 14:26).

In order for God to energize inspirational thoughts of remembrance, those thoughts must be initially received and retained. These are the thoughts of God that have come from

the written Word of God or from what God has told you previously. Often verses of Scripture "pop up" into your mind as God's Word is being shared with someone. Perhaps you have experienced this. Suddenly, seemingly out of nowhere, a Scripture or thought comes to your mind. This is God reminding you. He could call a song to remembrance or a quiet suggestion to pray for someone. These are things you already have been exposed to. God does not have to reveal them to you and teach you these things anew because you already know them. God simply energizes the gift of the holy spirit and the spirit will bring the thought to the top of your mind.

Often in the quietness of prayer, such thoughts come to mind as: "I love you"; "Forget it and move on"; or "Fear not!" These are thoughts from God's Word already retained in the mind. This is the energizing of God bringing His Word and thoughts back to your remembrance. This is just as much God's Word as when He said, "Let there be light," or when He spoke to the prophets of old. An inspirational reminder from God is just as vital as revelation. Accept these quiet reminders of His love and goodness. This is your joy, privilege, and benefit of fellowshiping with your heavenly Father. God energizes thoughts in your mind by reminding you of things that you already know. This is inspiration; it is God working within you to bring things to your remembrance.

God also tells you things that you have not previously known. This is called revelation.

God Teaches You—Revelation

God energizes thoughts within believers by teaching previously unknown information. Since this teaching indicates the revealing of previously unknown knowledge, this is called revelation.

For I neither received it of man, neither was I taught it, but by the revelation of Jesus Christ (Galatians 1:12).

"Revelation" is the Greek word *apokalupsis.* It is comprised of two words: *apo* "to take away" and *kalupto,* "the veil or cover." Literally, revelation is where the veil or cover is removed to "reveal" the unknown item. Revelation is the unveiling of previously unseen information. Literally, the veil is removed so something can be seen for the first time. This is what happens when God energizes the gift of the holy spirit with previously unknown information.

Which things also we speak, not in the words which man's wisdom teacheth, but which the Holy Ghost teacheth; comparing spiritual things with spiritual (1 Corinthians 2:13).

The context of First Corinthians 2 shows that God reveals spiritual truths to man. When this happens, the person must compare the spiritual things that have been revealed to the spiritual things in the written Word of God. This is a fundamental (and primary) truth concerning spiritually revealed information: It must always be compared to the written Scriptures.

These "new" spiritual words must flow in accordance with the written Scriptures. This information may augment the written Word of God, but it will never contradict it. As soon as new information is received, the Christian believer's first responsibility is to take this information and compare it to the written Scriptures. The truth recorded in the Scriptures is that God cannot lie (see Heb. 6:18). This also means that He cannot contradict Himself. First Corinthians 2:13 explains that spiritually-received information must be compared to the truth of the written Scriptures.

God also works within His people to give them spiritual understanding.

For this cause we also, since the day we heard it, do not cease to pray for you, and to desire that ye might be filled with the knowledge of His will in all wisdom and spiritual understanding (Colossians 1:9).

Spiritual understanding is what God may give to His people so they can know "why." This is "background" information that God gives so they can see the whole picture. This may not always appear as "new" information, but as insight into "why" things are happening. God many times reveals information that helps to firm up a believer's standing. What is under a believer's standing is "understanding."

Consider what I say; and the Lord give thee understanding in all things (2 Timothy 2:7).

Spiritual knowledge, wisdom, and understanding all come through the spirit of God. This information is not natural knowledge, it can only be learned from God.

But the natural man [of body and soul, that does not have the holy spirit] *receiveth not the things of the Spirit of God: for they are foolishness unto him: neither can he know them, because they are spiritually discerned* (1 Corinthians 2:14).

A Christian believer has the holy spirit, which is an avenue of learning the natural man of only body and soul does not have. The believer has the holy spirit, a connection with God, through which he may learn the things freely given by God. He learns these deeper truths as they are taught by God through the holy spirit.

Luke 12:12 shows that God teaches His children by enlightening their minds with information when they need it.

For the Holy Ghost shall teach you in the same hour [immediately] *what ye ought to say* (Luke 12:12).

The Father reveals necessary information to His children when they need it. If the information is already present within the believer, He simply brings it to remembrance. If information is not present, He can reveal to His children what they need to know through the spirit.

Let us therefore, as many as be perfect, be thus minded: and if in any thing ye be otherwise minded, God shall reveal even this unto you (Philippians 3:15).

Since God is the loving Father, would He not correct and direct His children? God will reveal to His children when they are not following the right way. He could do this by inspirationally reminding His child of a previously known Scripture, or He could reveal "new" information that would keep His child from going down a wrong path.

Illustrations of revelation are throughout the Bible. Information about future events, specific ministering situations, details about how to carry out what needs to be done, or dealing with evil spirits are only a few examples of this kind of information. The expanse and detail of this kind of information is unlimited because it comes from the omniscient God. The major consideration of revelation is not the category, but the source. That it comes from God makes it always reliable and accurate.

God may energize revelation at any time. Sometimes He gives it without being asked for it. Other times it is requested and He graciously gives it. Regardless of how or when revelation is given, it is based upon the goodness and grace of God.

There may be times when the child of God asks his heavenly Father for information that is not needed. This would be similar to a child wanting something from his parents that he does not need. Often, just as a child acts when he is denied a request, so a child of God may respond toward God also. He may pout when denied a request. Pouting, pleading, or badgering usually does not change the mind of an earthly parent. It certainly will not change the heavenly Father's decision either. A child may at times badger his parents into changing their minds, but God is not so whimsical. A man cannot change God's will by his own determination. God cannot be emotionally coaxed into giving information that is not necessary. All revelation comes by God's decision to give it, according to a person's need and not just his desire.

God has foreknowledge. His determination of what is really needed exceeds the finite scope of man. God's scope of events is far, far greater than the senses' mind. God has knowledge of the future; He always has matters fully covered. God is not only all-knowing, but He is all-loving, too.

If you ask for information and do not receive it, it is because God has another approach planned and a more loving and convenient way to handle the matter. If God decides to not reveal to you what you think you need to know, rest assured that He has it fully covered because His love covers all. Do not be insulted if you are not personally involved in the process. Let God be God. There is no way to squeak revelation out of Him if it is not His will to tell. Be thankful and peaceful to know that at least one member of the family has perfect understanding and foreknowledge. Let patience have her perfect work (see Jas. 1:4).

Once it is accepted that God is working in you and talking to you, the most commonly asked question therefore becomes, "How do I know when it is God speaking to me or when it is just me thinking and talking to myself?"

Recognizing the Voice of God Within You

The old saying, "God works in mysterious ways," does not apply to how He teaches His people to recognize when He speaks to them.

> *(Now the man Moses was very meek* [humble], *above all the men which were upon the face of the earth.) ... And He* [God] *said, Hear now My words: If there be a prophet among you, I the Lord will make Myself known unto him in a vision, and will speak unto him in a dream. My servant Moses is not so, who is faithful in all Mine house. With him will I speak mouth to mouth, even apparently* [clearly seen], *and not in dark speeches* [riddles]*; and the similitude* [likeness] *of the Lord shall he behold...* (Numbers 12:3,6-8).

This statement of how God worked with Moses shows how He works with all humble people. God did not make Moses guess when He talked to him. He showed Himself plainly to Moses. He did not speak in hidden riddles; nor did He make Moses wonder when He spoke to him. He spoke mouth to mouth to His servant Moses. Would He do less for His child?

In learning to recognize the voice of God, remember these Scriptures regarding Moses and be humble. God knows if you do not recognize His voice. Be humble and ask Him to help you. He will show you how. Especially remember that God is your Father. He is not trying to play hide and seek. He is your Father and does not work in mystery. If He plainly showed Himself to His servant Moses, how much more plainly will He show Himself to you, His child?

I remember the first time I was exposed to teachings concerning revelation. I was upset that no one taught me to recognize what God's voice sounded like. Yet the more I studied the Word of God and practiced recognizing the presence of God within me, the more I realized the only one who could truly teach me was God Himself. From time to time people come to me and ask me to teach them to walk by the spirit. I am very humbled when asked, but the response is always the same. "I may be able to help you learn about it, but only God can truly teach you how to do it."

Remember to be strong in grace. To hear from God is not something that you have to earn. God wants to talk to you. He lives inside of you and knows your heart. You are His child and He is your Father. He is the one Whom you want to recognize. Let Him show you how to listen to Him. Isn't it reasonable that He is the one who will help you understand this?

Jesus Christ, the true master of walking and talking with God, teaches this:

Howbeit when He, the Spirit of truth, is come, He will guide you into all truth: for He shall not speak of Himself; but whatsoever He shall hear, that shall He speak: and He will shew you things to come (John 16:13).

The "Spirit of truth" is the gift of the holy spirit as it functions within you to teach you truth. God speaks to the spirit of truth, and it speaks to your mind. The gift of the holy spirit does not speak of itself. It speaks what God energizes it to speak. God tells the spirit, then the spirit tells your mind. When the spirit of truth within you speaks, it speaks only what it hears from God. The spirit within you is the connection to God.

A relationship between a radio station and a radio offers a good analogy. The radio station sends a signal; the radio receives the signal. The radio does not speak of itself. It only transmits what it receives. Likewise, God sends the signal and the spirit within you receives it. The spirit of God within you does not speak of itself; it receives what God sends. After the spirit of God within you receives the information, the spirit of truth tells your mind what it hears from God. What the spirit of God within you hears is what it speaks.

Accepting that God is speaking to you means accepting that the spirit of God within you is receiving information from God and telling your mind. You have a source of information rather than just your own intellect that reminds you and teaches you. Recognizing when the spirit speaks to you as opposed to when your own mind is speaking is the dilemma that needs to be resolved.

The previous chapter, "Stay Your Mind on God," explains how the mind operates. A brief review of that material is in order to fully comprehend the dilemma of "thought sorting." First, the mind is the organ of perception. Its job is to receive and store information. The mind is an organ and, as such, does not distinguish between natural or spiritual information. Also, the mind's function is to receive the information, not to sort it. Sorting the different kinds of information is your job.

Again the obvious question becomes, "How do I know when a thought is an energized thought from God or when it is just me listening to myself?"

A common problem in discerning a natural thought from a spiritual thought is believers trying to listen for a distinction in sound. Since both natural and spiritual thoughts come into the mind and finally arrive at a common point of awareness, both will "sound" the same. For example, if you step on a thumbtack, when the information comes to your awareness, it is your mind giving you physical information. If God tells your spirit and your spirit tells your mind that it is going to rain tomorrow, that information comes to your mind and your mind tells you. Both pieces of information will sound the same because they come to the same mind and the same mind tells you. It is the source from which the information comes that is different, not the sound.

When God works in you, He uses the same facilities to communicate to you as your brain and five senses do. In the spiritual realm, God tells the spirit that is in you to tell your mind. In the physical realm, your body or five senses tells your brain and your brain tells your mind. Obviously, the information "sounds" the same. The mind is simply the organ of mental perception; it does not differentiate between the sources of the information.

To distinguish between your own thoughts and the energized words of God, do not listen for a difference in sound. Instead, *you* watch for the source from which the thought comes.

For the prophecy came not in old time by the will of man: but holy men of God spake as they were moved by the Holy Ghost (2 Peter 1:21).

The prophecy of written Scriptures came by God telling the spirit within a man of God, then the spirit told the mind and the man knew it. This is exactly how God communicates in you. The major point in this verse to consider is not what the word sounds like, but where it came from. The information came when the men were "moved by the Holy Ghost."

(An interesting note for individuals of grammatical inclination: Usages of the holy spirit related with verbs in the passive voice are very "revealing." The subject is "passive" when he or she is acted upon by God as He energizes the spirit. This is the usage in Second Peter 1:21. The subject, holy men, were passive and then were acted upon by the holy spirit. In other words, the spirit of God moved first and acted upon them; the spirit was the initiator of the action. Other examples of this are in Matthew 4:1, Luke 4:1, Romans 8:14, Second Corinthians 3:18, Ephesians 3:16, and First Peter 3:18. These examples show the active energizing from the spirit as it acts upon a passive subject. The same truth of a passive verb is indicated when the Word of God states that "Jesus was moved *with* or *by* compassion.")

When a thought comes to mind and you wonder if it was God speaking, ask yourself this: "What moved me to think that?" Ask yourself, "Did I originate this thought? Did it come from my five senses? Was it prompted by my logic? Or was it energized outside of my own will?"

Thoughts coming from God come by the will of God. Thoughts generated by the mind itself come from the will of man. All information from God comes by the will of God, not the will of man. Instead of listening for a distinction in sound, watch for it to come from a different source.

For example, it is difficult to tell who sent a letter by the sound it makes when it falls into the mailbox. Do not listen to the sound; instead, pick up the letter and look at the return address. In distinguishing between thoughts from God or from your own mind, pick up the letter, or thought, and ask yourself, "What is the postmark on that thought? Where did it come from?"

Spiritually-energized thoughts in your mind come from the will of God. If a thought within you did not come *from* the will of God, then it is not spiritually energized by God.

According to Second Peter 1:21, prophecy, the revelation of God in Scripture, did not come by man willing the thoughts to come to his mind. Rather, it came by holy men of

God speaking as they were moved *by* the holy spirit. This is similar to the coming of Jesus Christ, the Word in the flesh.

Which [Who, Jesus Christ] *were* [was] *born, not of blood, nor of the will of the flesh, nor of the will of man, but of God* (John 1:13).

Jesus Christ did not come by the will of man. No one dreamed up the Messiah. Mary did not close her eyes and by mentally picturing a fertilization within her womb, conceive the Messiah. Jesus Christ came by the direct action of the will and choice of God. God moved according to His own will and energized Jesus Christ into existence.

This is the same way God works within you. You cannot close your eyes, grunt, strain, and make God talk to you. All information from God comes from God energizing the information into existence. It comes by the will, action, and energizing of God.

Watch how Jesus Christ walked:

Then was Jesus led up of [by] *the Spirit into the wilderness...* (Matthew 4:1).

Did Jesus Christ will this thought Himself? No. The spirit of God in Him told Him to go into the wilderness. Where did the thought of going into the wilderness originate? Did it come from the mind of Jesus or as the spirit told Him? It is that simple. God told Jesus to go into the wilderness. He was led *by* the spirit into the wilderness, just as holy men of God spoke as they were moved *by* the spirit.

So, although thoughts from the mind and thoughts from the spirit of God may sound the same, the origin is different.

Do not listen for a distinction in sound. Look for thoughts that come from the will of God and not from your own will.

Watch and be ready. An energized thought from God will come from a different direction and source. It will not come from your own will. The energized thoughts from God will not be willed by you. You may have asked for the information, but if God gives it, it will not come from your own will. Information from God is not brought to pass by the will of man. God works in you according to His own decision to give information.

For example, I once had a job of securing a building by locking all the doors. One day, as I reflected upon the job after I was finished, I began wondering if I had locked one particular door. The more I thought about it, the more I convinced myself that God had told me that I had not. When I went to see if it was God Who told me about the door, the door was already locked. I had willed the thought myself.

Unfortunately, this is a great pitfall of endeavoring to walk by the spirit. This is "self-willed determination" instead of "God-energized revelation." People may take a thought that came by their own will and try to convince themselves that God said it. Sometimes the person begins to tell himself (and maybe even others) that he has heard from the Lord. As sincere as this is, the individual is walking by his own senses and will.

The word *will* in John 1:13 and other Scriptures is the Greek word *thelema*. This type of will simply means "to desire." Another great question to ask yourself when determining if God spoke to you or if you conjured up the thought yourself is, "Is this thought my desire or is this thought

God's desire?" Ask yourself, "Did I will this thought by my own desires or did He will it by His desires?"

Another time while working at the job I described earlier, I was sitting reading a book when, suddenly, a thought came to my mind that someone needed to get into the building, which was already locked. I recognized that I had not consciously willed the thought myself. I asked God if the thought was from Him. He said, "Yes, go to the back door of the kitchen." When I got there, the door was locked and a delivery man was standing outside wanting to get in. The thought had arrived from a different direction than my own will—it came from the will of God.

It is a great accomplishment to accept that God works in you and talks to you. Learning to recognize God's voice and direction is an exciting adventure also. It is exciting because God can teach you. You have a personal tutor through the spirit of Christ in you.

Howbeit when He, the Spirit of truth, is come, He will guide you into all truth: for He shall not speak of Himself; but whatsoever He shall hear, that shall He speak: and He will shew you things to come (John 16:13).

God will guide you into understanding His voice through the instruction of holy spirit. Should it come as a surprise that one of the functions of holy spirit is to teach us *how* to walk in the spirit? *Guide* literally means "will lead you into the way." God will lead you into understanding His voice. If God is the guide, then how difficult can this be?

On numerous occasions I have had individuals ask me if a thought that they had was God talking to them or just their own minds. My response is, "Why ask me? Ask God. Isn't He the one you want to talk to anyway? Eventually you'll have to handle it with Him. Why not start now?"

In rebuttal, some have said, "How am I supposed to get God to teach me if I do not know how to listen to Him?" The answer is that the Teacher is smarter than the pupil and more desirous to teach than the pupil is to learn. Ask Him. Your efforts will be well-rewarded by gaining a personal relationship with Him and recognizing God's voice when He speaks to you.

God will teach you. He knows if you know very little Scripture. He even knows if you have tried to build an intellectual relationship with Him through the knowledge of the Scriptures. He knows if you have been a vacillating disciple like Peter or a henchman like Paul. He knows your shortcomings and your abilities. He knows all about you and still loves you. He is your Father. He will teach you.

God Is Your Father; He Teaches You

Have you ever observed a parent working with a child? The parent is down on bent knees speaking directly to the child in terms that the child can understand. Have you watched parents coaxing a child to walk? They plead with outstretched arms and beckon for the child to just try. This is how God works with you. He is not waiting for you to leap out of your chair and run across the room. He wants you to make a simple effort. He will not scold you if you fall. He is imploring you to make a decision to walk. When you make a move, if you fall, He will catch you.

He is your Father. God will work with you. Ask Him to help you. He will teach you.

As mentioned earlier in this chapter, one of the greatest misconceptions people have regarding the New Testament is that God still deals with people as He did in the Old Testament. In the Old Testament, people were servants—their relationship with God was based upon their works. In the New Testament, believers are children—their relationship with God is based upon grace. Servants are treated differently than sons. A father teaches a child over and over again until he learns. A servant is instructed and then expected to perform. God is our Father. He is more interested that we learn to fellowship with Him than He is concerned about what we can do for Him.

For ye have not received the spirit of bondage again to fear; but ye have received the Spirit of adoption [sonship which can never be lost], *whereby we cry, Abba, Father. The Spirit* [God] *itself* [Himself] *beareth witness with our spirit, that we are the children of God* (Romans 8:15-16).

God Shall Direct Your Path

The attitude that children of God hold in their own hearts about God greatly determines their success in learning to walk and talk with Him. God wants to help His children. He is patient and wants His children to trust Him.

Trust in the Lord with all thine heart; and lean not unto thine own understanding (Proverbs 3:5).

Can you imagine a parent who has the means to help a child and does not? Likewise, can you imagine a humble child of God asking Him for some help, and God not helping him? Proverbs 3:6 speaks loudly about this.

In all thy ways acknowledge Him, and He shall direct thy paths (Proverbs 3:6).

This verse needs to be diligently observed. This verse says that if you acknowledge God and ask Him for direction, then He absolutely *shall* direct you. Can you imagine a child asking a father a question and the father ignoring it and even refusing to reply? Proverbs 3:6 needs to be applied and accepted the same as Philippians 2:13 does. Say it over and over again. This verse does not say that God might direct your path. This is God speaking; He cannot lie. If you acknowledge Him, He *shall absolutely* direct your paths.

For God to direct your path, He must communicate to you in terms that you understand. Parents work with their children from infancy through adolescence to adulthood to make sure their children understand exactly what they are saying. Would God your Father do less? Since the Word of God promises that God absolutely shall direct your path, then He must communicate with you on a level that you understand.

This is pertinent information, especially in the early stages of learning to listen to God. Since God is all-knowing, He obviously knows if you are not sure about hearing from Him. He is not shocked when you say to Him, "Okay, Father, I think that I heard from You, but I am not exactly sure. Could you help me a little more by showing me this in another way?"

Can you imagine God getting upset because you need additional confirmation? Can you imagine an earthly dad getting upset if his child did not understand exactly what he said? Would not an earthly dad be more than glad to offer additional explanation rather than have his child guess at what he meant? Would he rather give a confirmation or have the child walk in ignorance?

Asking for a confirmation is simply saying, "Would you please bring this thing around another way just so that I can be sure?" All you are asking is for God to show it to you from a different angle. Do not teachers usually say, "Let me put it another way"? If airline companies are inclined to give confirmations, then surely the God of all love is also.

For example, a young lady was painting a picture. When she arrived at a place where she did not know which color to use to paint a particular object, she quietly, in the stillness of her own heart, asked God. She asked, "Father, what color should I use?" God replied, "Magenta." She was somewhat taken back by the simplicity and quickness of His response. She then said, "Father, You know me. I need to be sure. Could You show me another way?" God said to her, "Look out the window." As she turned her head, she saw a magenta-colored car passing by. God then said to her, "Do you understand now?"

As beautiful and as simple as this experience was, it became even better the next time the lady asked God what color to use to paint something. When she asked, God told her and she did not need for it to be confirmed. Even more important than choosing a correct color, when God would say to her, "I love you," she did not doubt, wonder, or question where the thought came from. She had learned to recognize the voice of her Father through a confirmation.

Since God is concerned about directing your path, He will not be displeased if you need additional clarification when He tells you something. He desires to communicate with you and to teach you to recognize when He is speaking to you. He does not become annoyed when you need a little extra help. He is not just your boss; He is your Father. He is not grading you—just helping you. If you need a confirmation of the information, ask Him for one.

This is why the most fundamental point to remember is that God is your loving Father. He is not an impatient tutor. He wants to develop a wonderful relationship with you. This is His idea, not yours. He is more willing and able to communicate than you are. "Ask and ye shall receive." (See John 16:24.)

Consider these points:

1. When you pray, do you pause and give God a chance to talk?

2. Do you *expect* to hear from Him when you ask? Remember to ask in faith.

3. Having faith that God talks to you is to expect that God will speak to you.

4. When God speaks to you, or even when you think that it might be Him speaking to you, write down the thought verbatim. After you write it down, do the following:

First, consider the source. Did it come from your own mental associations? Did it come from human origins or did it come by the will of God?

Second, does it agree with Scripture? God cannot lie. He could *never* contradict Himself. His revealed Word to you is as much His Word as John 3:16. Revelation may be thought of as what is written between the lines of the Bible. He did not need to tell you everything in the Scriptures; He gave you the holy spirit whereby He could supply the rest. What He tells you will *never* contradict the written Word of God.

Third, do you understand what He said? If not, then ask God for a confirmation. God primarily wants fellowship—not just a job to be done. He wants to communicate with you. He wants you to understand His voice. If you are not sure something came from Him, ask Him to show it to you in a different way. He will communicate with you on the level of your understanding. Eventually, as you learn the way He works within you, you will need fewer confirmations. He knows this. Do not be afraid to ask. Remember this even after you have begun to recognize when He speaks to you. If you need some extra help, just ask. This is His idea. He started this because He wants it.

Fourth, carry out what He says. If it is a specific direction to you, *do it.* If it is information or comforting words, your action is simply to believe it. If there is an action to take—simply do it.

Do all things without murmurings and disputings (Philippians 2:14).

God is at work within you. He is your loving Father and patient Teacher. As you pray and talk to Him, be patient and give Him a chance to respond. He will inspirationally warm your heart and bless you with reminders of the great things He has done for you already. He will also direct your paths with previously unknown information. Do not be surprised when you hear from Him specifically what to do. Do not be surprised when He tells you to do something for someone else. Just do what He says to do!

In all your ways acknowledge Him, and He *shall* direct your path.

You Don't Have to Be Smart to Walk With God. Just accept that He works within you.

The main strand in the "braid" of the simple walk with God is to accept that He works within you. Weave this together with being strong in grace, being humble, and having a stayed mind on God. Ask God. He will teach you.

Stay simple. Be strong in grace. Be humble. Stay your mind on God. Accept that He works within you. Ask God. He will teach you.

Summary

To walk and talk with God is His idea. We learned this from His Word. This process is not complicated because God designed it as the basis for fellowship with His children. It is simple because He invented it. If walking and talking with God were complicated, it would contradict His nature of love.

The simplicity of this relationship is available because God chooses to work within you. All information comes by His grace and willingness to give. He provides the energizing and the power within you; you provide the willingness and humility to listen and obey.

Remember, keeping it simple means to braid many things into one. Take the strands of grace, humility, and the stayed mind on God in one hand. In the other hand, take the strand of accepting that God works within you. Weave them together with the knowledge that God is your loving Father and that He is your Teacher.

These closing Scriptures are from the great prayer in Ephesians 1. This is not only the prayer that we are to pray for each other, but also God's desire and prayer for us. This great prayer summarizes the previous teaching of God's desire to reveal Himself to you.

> *That the God of our Lord Jesus Christ, the Father of glory, may give unto you the spirit of wisdom and revelation in the knowledge* [acknowledgment] *of Him:* [that] *the eyes of your* [spiritual] *understanding being enlightened; that ye may know what is the hope of His calling, and what the riches of the glory of His inheritance in the saints, and what is the exceeding greatness of His power to us-ward who believe, according to the working* [energizing] *of His mighty power* (Ephesians 1:17-19).

God desires to reveal Himself to you through His spirit within you. He quietly energizes thoughts into your conscious awareness as your Father to enlighten your understanding concerning the riches He has made available to you, His child. He wants you to know that He energizes great power in your life.

How humbling it is to discover that God chooses to work within you! This is His decision, and He faithfully performs what He has promised.

Walking and talking with God and knowing Him is His idea.

You did not invent the idea; He did.

He provides the power; you provide the willingness.

God wants you to know Him.

He will reveal His ways to you through His Word.
He will reveal Himself to you through the spirit.
When you pray, always give God a chance to talk.
Keep it simple.
Be strong in grace.
Be humble.
Stay your mind on God.
Accept that God is working within you.
God is your Father. Ask Him to help you.
You Don't Have to Be Smart to Walk With God because *He is.*

"Exercising Spiritual Authority"

A Biblical Presentation of the Power of God

And my speech and my preaching was not with enticing words of man's wisdom, but in demonstration of the Spirit and of power: that your faith should not stand in the wisdom of men, but in the power of God (1 Corinthians 2:4-5).

Rev. Dale Sides travels extensively teaching classes on how to demonstrate God's power. All nine evidences of the gift of the holy spirit (see 1 Cor. 12:8-10) are covered, with the emphasis on each person manifesting "gifts of healing" as operated by revelation. This is not just a teaching session, but practical instruction in exercising the spiritual authority that God has given to every Christian believer.

For more details, class schedules, and bookings, call or write:

The Believers' Bible Camp, Inc.
Rt. 4 Box 34A
Bedford, VA 24523
(703) 586-5813

SECRETS OF THE MOST HOLY PLACE

by Don Nori.

Here is a prophetic parable you will read again and again. The winds of God are blowing, drawing you to His Life within the Veil of the Most Holy Place. There you begin to see as you experience a depth of relationship your heart has yearned for. This book is a living, dynamic experience with God!

TPB-182p. ISBN 1-56043-076-1
Retail $8.99

COMMUNION WITH GOD
by Mark and Patti Virkler.

This is the most practical book on the market today teaching Christians specifically how to experience dialog with Almighty God. Teaching the use of vision, intuitive heart flow, and journaling, this book will bring you to the place where you can daily record page after page of what the Lord is saying to you.

TPB-224p. ISBN 1-56043-012-5
Retail $17.99
(8³/₈" X 11")

FROM THE FATHER'S HEART
by Charles Slagle.

This is a beautiful look at the Father's heart. This sensitive selection includes short love notes and letters, as well as prophetic words from God to those among His children who diligently seek Him. Be ready for a time with God as you read this book.

TPB-160p. ISBN 0-914903-82-9
Retail $7.99